KILLER
EXECUTIONS
AND
SCRUBBED DECKS

An Outside-the-Box Look at Obnoxious Advertising and Marketing Jargon

Dan Goldgeier

ACKNOWLEDGMENTS

Special thanks to the folks at Talent Zoo (TalentZoo.com). Since 2002 they've given me space on their site to ruminate on the state of the advertising business, saving me from thousands of dollars in therapy bills.

No one dissected the idiosyncrasies and absurdities of the English language better than George Carlin. So I dedicate this book to him.

BUCKETS OF CONTENT

ADVERTISING ISN'T BUSINESS. IT'S WAR!

We're all combatants now, or so you'd think if you spent a day in the ad industry. Frankly, it's too easy to use war as a metaphor for business. It gives everything a false sense of urgency; it implies that in every business decision there are outright victors and losers. But I suppose that in a world of "Hurry, supplies are limited!" urgency is normal. Besides, a little bomb throwing never hurt anyone...

KILLER

Describing any great ad as "killer" always perplexes me. If an ad is a killer, well, does it mean the ad's "target" would be rendered dead by watching or reading the ad? Are we talking about advertising or quail hunting? Killer diseases are bad. Killer bees are bad. Serial killers like the Son of Sam are bad. Why are killer ads good?

EXECUTIONS

In advertising agencies around the world, thousands of unsuspecting, innocent-looking ads are executed every day. An "execution" of an idea means a finished version of the idea. Just like variations of the death penalty, there are many ways to execute an idea.

Since there are some nuances to these warlike phrases, here are some points to remember. Or, "bullet points":

- *Any ad can be executed, but killers are usually executed well.*

- *An ad is also "killed" when someone decides it isn't going to reach the public. So you can have a killer ad killed by a client before you get a chance to execute it.*

- *At any moment, your executions may be killed at random by people you've never met for reasons that don't make sense.*

4

HARD-HITTING

I once had a client who continually requested that ads be more "hard-hitting." This meant inserting more exclamation points, more use of warnings like "DON'T MISS OUT!" and of course, more starbursts and snipes in the layouts. The result? My ads were hard-hitting, but they weren't killer. Many clients believe hard-hitting ads work and I think I know why. Ads deemed to be "hard-hitting" leave the audience staggered, but still physically able to buy something. However, an audience killed by "killer" ads is dead and can't use their credit cards.

- *Killer ads tend to win more industry praise than hard-hitting ads.*

- *Ads with copy that consists of bullet points generally aren't considered killer ads, either.*

#BadCopywriterWisdom
Life is a list of bullet points.
Are yours in the right order?

TARGET

Advertising generally isn't intended for humans. It's intended for a target, which is a group of humans. The target could be broad or narrow, such as, "Our target is men ages 18-34 who are desperately looking to get laid." In order to reach your target, you may be asked to target them with targeted ads. If you're lucky, you might nail the target, and see an explosion in sales.

- *Marketers, in turn, have sales targets they need to hit. So they're really hoping your targeted ads cause the target to buy enough product to hit the sales target.*

- *Is it better to target your target with hard-hitting ads or killer ads? This is actually a decades-old debate within the ad industry. Or rather, a raging battle.*

WAR ROOM

Often commandeered for a new business pitch or new campaign, this is a room at the agency where everyone gathers to discuss the target, the plan of attack, and show all the ads in consideration to determine which ones are killers, which should be killed, and which should be executed. War rooms also tend to be littered with junk food containers and soda cans, which could also kill you — although it's more of a slow death.

FALL ON YOUR SWORD

Let's say you really want to execute something killer, but your boss or client doesn't care for it and isn't prepared for the carnage that may result. You may decide to fall on your sword. In other words, you will fight for the work you believe in, and possibly risk committing career suicide. Yes, when it comes to defending the artistic and aesthetic integrity of banner ads and taglines, it may very well be a matter of life or death.

It's entirely possible that advertising isn't war. Rather, it's a sports contest.

If many different creative teams get the same assignment, it's considered a "jump ball." Hopefully, this will help the agency and client "move the ball forward" even if some teams "drop the ball." And regular communication is essential, so we continually "touch base" with each other and eventually "circle back" to see how far we've progressed. Remember, advertising is a collaborative business and there's no "I" in team (although there is an "m" and an "e").

AROUND THE AD AGENCY

Often when I've told people that I work in an advertising agency, they're impressed. Agency life seems like another world to them. Maybe they've seen *Mad Men*. Or *What Women Want*. Or *Bosom Buddies*. And like many professions, the ad world has a vernacular all its own that outsiders may not understand.

Getting into the advertising or marketing business is often a mystifying process. You don't need a degree. You don't need a formal resume. Sometimes, you don't even need pants. But the way advertising professionals speak doesn't mirror the rest of the business world. It's definitely a way of determining, "Hey, are you one of us?" So if you find yourself amongst ad people, here are some terms that'll help you fit right in.

(This section is especially useful if you're a young creative building a portfolio. Trust me, it'll come in handy when it's time to show that book full of killer executions.)

SHOP

Advertising agencies are commonly referred to as "shops." This term has an old-world feel, as if ad people were craftsmen and artisans like cobblers or blacksmiths. But in my experience, clients tend to dictate what they want and get it exactly how they want it, the way Meg Ryan ordered food in *When Harry Met Sally*. Maybe we should refer to an ad agency not as a "shop," but as a "diner."

- *Synonyms include "studio" and "boutique," which usually mean "we're all crammed in one big room."*

BOOK

This word has a strange dual meaning: It describes both a creative portfolio of work and, more oddly, a magazine. The first time I heard a Creative Director refer to home improvement magazines as "shelter books" I nearly pissed in my pants from laughing so hard. A term like that sounds ridiculous, but it's common usage. So if magazines are "books," what do we call actual hard-bound books? Ironically, in this age of online portfolios and tablet-based magazine apps, even a book isn't exactly a book anymore.

- *For a creative person in advertising, a book is never finished. You're always supposed to be working on it. A book can be rough and lack polish, like a worn pair of shoes. But unlike a worn pair of shoes, a rough book lacking polish won't get you anywhere.*

10

KILLER BOOK

A killer book is neither a "killer" nor a "book." It's a great portfolio. Calling it a "killer book" is, of course, a rather odd phrase. A biography of Charles Manson is a killer book. A bomb-making manual is a killer book. So why is a portfolio considered one?

PRODUCED

An idea that gets "produced" means the ad actually appears somewhere in the real media world like on-air, in print, or online. Producing an ad means you've brought it to life. What confuses me is in regular English, "execute" means "to put to death" while "produce" means "to bring into existence." In advertising, though, it's perfectly acceptable to use the two words together, which makes for some bizarre English.

- *An ad that is produced may not be the best possible execution, and your executions may not be well-produced.*

- *You can produce executions and execute what you'd like to produce. Either way, it's all good!*

#BadCopywriterWisdom
**Life is a template.
How are you formatting yours?**

EDGY

Lots of advertising people tout the need for "edgy" ideas. But when anything — a physical object or an idea — has an edge, someone is bound to get cut. The moral here is that if you go to present an edgy idea to a client, bring some tourniquets. Remember: Edgy ideas are not always killer ideas. And as we discussed earlier, if you fall on your sword for an edgy idea, you might be the one who gets killed. Or fired.

- *Innovative Ideas may also be described as "cutting edge" or "bleeding edge." Genius must be painful, I suppose.*

#BadCopywriterWisdom
Life is cloud-based.
What are you storing on yours?

CREATIVE BRIEF

Ideally, a creative brief should be both creative and brief. Many are neither.

LEGS

I'm not talking about the legs on our bodies. If someone says, "That idea has legs," they believe it has the potential to run anywhere, in many forms, and incessantly. Is that what we want? Perhaps it's better to say a good idea has both a sperm and an egg, so it can be reproduced many ways and live on. Regardless, we don't need more ideas with "legs." We need more ideas with heart. Or brains.

- *If an idea has legs, you may be able to produce many executions for a long time. And putting all those produced killer executions into your book may land you a great gig doing edgy work in a hot shop.*

BLOW IT OUT

Let's say you think your idea has legs. Great! Now you can "blow it out." Does that mean blowing out the legs? Sounds like you're turning the idea into an amputee. We can expand on ideas. Or build on them. But blowing them out? Use this phrase at your peril. Because you could be blowing out something that, upon close examination, really blows or sucks. And that could get messy.

- *Another synonym for this is "flesh out." So you could flesh out an idea by giving it legs. It's a little more life-affirming to say it that way, I suppose.*

CONTENT

I get why this one's used so much, and I use it too. Since the Internet has given us almost infinite space to work in, "content" is a catch-all word to describe anything from videos and blog posts to tweets and ads. Before the Internet, we used to call much of this type of work "collateral." And in the absence of another singular word to describe many things, "content" works. The problem is, "content" sounds so undefined it might be referring to a pile of amorphous shit and pus that goes into a large container. Like a 55-gallon drum that needs to be filled. "Content" is a cold, unemotional word. Maybe that's why so much content is void of ideas or quality.

- *Because content is such a mushy word, there's all kinds of it. Long-form, short-form, and my favorite: snackable. Like a bag of Cheetos, most snackable content is devoid of nutrition yet we can't stop ourselves. "Bet you can't click on just one listicle!"*

- *Content is also self-perpetuating. Many people make content about content aimed at other content makers. It often feels like a big circle jerk. Or as some people would call it, sticky content.*

#BadCopywriterWisdom
Life is an OS upgrade.
Is your app updated?

STORY

People love stories. Some people love telling them and most of us love hearing them. So brands, marketers, and ad agency people are embracing the mantra of "storytelling." That's OK, even if it's incorrect or overused. But I find it obnoxious when people use the word "story" as a concept the way snotty, wanna-be aristocrats use "sport" instead of "sports." I'd like to see a news story that talks about the demise of people who talk about "story."

- *It's not enough to be a "brand storyteller" these days. Telling ain't selling, you know. Hence, the rise of self-professed "storymakers," "storydoers," "storycrafters," and "storysellers." There's nothing new about mashing two words up in an attempt to make advertising sound more impressive. In other words, I've heard this story before.*

CALL TO ACTION

It's not enough to use advertising tell someone about a product or service. The goal is to get them to act — and do something they weren't planning on doing. "Call now." "Visit our website." "Head down to MattressLand for the Great Tent Event." Invariably, all calls to action have the same intent, which was expressed perfectly in *Goodfellas*: "Fuck you, pay me." Stick that on your next banner ad and I guarantee it'll jack up that 0.00001% response rate you'd ordinarily get.

NATIVE ADVERTISING

Supposedly, native advertising is any type of ad that blends in seamlessly to the media environment surrounding it. We used to call them "advertorials" and "infomercials" until we found new ways to toss advertising into social media sites or news aggregation sites like BuzzFeed. Sooner or later, we may discover that native advertising doesn't really have much value; it just gets in the way and needs to be marginalized. Which, unfortunately, is sort of like how we treated Native Americans.

#BadCopywriterWisdom
Life is iterative.
What version of yourself are you on?

DELIVERABLE

Actually, this is a bad one. A really bad one. Agencies often don't get paid for their general thinking or for proposing ideas that might improve a client's business, like beefing up customer service or retraining employees. No, ad agencies get paid for specific deliverables, like a pizza parlor. "Would you like a direct mail piece with everything in it and extra logos to go?" Because you can bill a client for that deliverable.

THE ASK

When did "ask" become a noun? "What's the ask?" It's meant to be a variation of "What's the objective?" or "What action do we want people to take?" The answer to the ask could be, "We want the creative team to work over the weekend redoing these banner ads" or "We want consumers to scan the QR code to receive $1 off their burrito." The ask is usually the wish, or more likely, the demand. My ask is different: I respectfully ask that you never use this wretched phrase.

SEASONED

This one is an employment-related term. When you've gotten some experience, now you're seasoned. You can look at this word in two ways. Basically, you're a cast iron pot and you've been in the fire. People toss some raw meat your way and with your seasoned abilities you can turn up the sizzle and cook up a great steak. Or you can look at yourself as a hearty meal with some flavor. In that case, "seasoned" is a horrible way to describe someone with experience. Because after that comes fried, eaten, and excreted.

#BadCopywriterWisdom
Life is customer-facing.
Who's buying what you're selling?

THINK OUTSIDE THE BOX

Every day, thousands of advertising and marketing people go to work in tall, rectangular office buildings, squeeze themselves into square elevators, ride up to an office where they sit in tiny cubicles encased by perpendicular walls, and get regularly shuttled into long, narrow conference rooms where they're routinely encouraged to "think outside the box." In this case, the "box" is a synonym for a conventional approach. Many creative people get inspiration in other places besides the office. So if you work in a steel and glass box, it's a good idea to walk outside the box once in a while in order to think outside the box.

- *A similar phrase is "push the envelope." Do you need to pick just one cliché? Perhaps not. Since one describes physical action and the other mental, it's entirely possible to push the envelope even if you think inside the box. Although people who overuse these phrases can't walk and chew gum at the same time.*

PAID MEDIA

Advertising.

WIDOWS & ORPHANS

More morbid terms, this time from the world of typography. A widow basically means a short line that's forced to go alone on its own column or page. An orphan is when there's a lone word on a line at the end of a... paragraph.

To the rest of the world, killers are mass murderers who often leave behind many widows and orphans. You'd think a so-called "killer book" would have lots of widows and orphans. But if you're a designer, your work won't be considered killer if it has widows and orphans. However, some people believe the craft of typography is dead. So don't be surprised at seeing so many widows and orphans left in its wake.

BUCKETS

Sometimes, during a brainstorm, the downpour of ideas becomes such a vast pool of genius that someone needs to mop it all up and place it into a number of categorized "buckets." Hopefully without spilling any of that brilliance.

- *There's always a stray idea or two that doesn't conveniently fit into a large bucket with lots of other ideas. These end up in the "Fuck It Bucket" and are usually never seen again.*

VIRAL

I don't know who first looked at their marketing budget and said, "Now, if only we could be as successful as Ebola or Herpes. Let's do something the great unwashed consumers could spread without more media dollars." Thus, viral marketing caught on. No actual viral campaign has spread quite like the mere concept of doing a viral marketing campaign has. There are even people who refer to a viral campaign's "infection rate," defined as the ease at which it can be forwarded and spread. I'm developing an immunity to viral marketing. I suspect most consumers are, too.

- *It's a bit of an open secret that most viral ideas don't spread by themselves. Often a brand or agency pays for advertising or publicity to make sure people come into contact with the viral idea. Really, it's the handiwork of some sick bastards.*

SCOPE CREEP

Looks bad, doesn't it? Pronounce this out loud. It even sounds bad, like "shell shock" or "Miley Cyrus." Basically, scope creep is what happens when an agency promises a client it'll produce deliverables A, B, and C, then the client comes back and asks for D, E, F, and G while not wanting to pay for more work or extend the deadline. Beware of scope creep, because once it takes root in your agency/client relationship you'll never get rid of it.

PROGRAMMATIC

Programmatic is problematic. Or so I hear. It's the new way online and other ads are bought: In bulk, by a computer, for the lowest rates, on a multitude of websites most people (including the media buyers) never visit. Simply put, it's another method to strip the humanity out of the advertising process. But if you want to remain relevant in the business today, you need to get with the program and use words like "programmatic" so you at least give the appearance of knowing what you're talking about. I wish we could deprogram ourselves of the instinct to talk like programmed robots.

CHECK-IN

"Hey! We just gave you the creative brief this morning! Let's check in at 4:00 to see your ideas, OK?" It sounds innocent enough, but the reality is that "check-ins" are meetings or quick chats often used to preempt or disrupt the normal flow of the creative process. Probably because the project timeline is so freakin' accelerated. Here's the problem — once account service, management, or clients get used to seeing creative ideas when they're half-baked, check-ins become an unbreakable habit. And to paraphrase an old cockroach trap commercial, once they check-in, they never, ever check out.

CURATION

Unless you're working in a museum or art gallery, you've got no business throwing this one around. It's merely a fancy-ass way of saying you're making decisions. Or you're picking out stuff you like. If you think a store can be curated, consider that Walmart plans their store layouts and merchandise mix down to the last shelf of baked beans. Are Walmart stores curated spaces? No. "Curation" is a pretentious word and so are the people who throw it around so liberally and incorrectly.

- *The phrase "content curation" is twice as pretentious and is uttered by people who take their job way too seriously. Lord knows I can't take them seriously.*

- *I'm writing this manuscript on Microsoft Word for Mac 2011. "Curation" is red-flagged on the spellchecker, which means Microsoft doesn't consider it a legitimate word either. Trust me, it's a rare moment when I'm in complete agreement with Microsoft.*

HACK

The short version: You don't want to be one. You want to be involved in one.

To a creative person, calling them a hack is a severe insult. It means they're washed-up (assuming they'd ever been out to sea), talentless, and only capable of churning out bad work. But a hack is also awesome. With its origins in the computer culture, many people hack to alter or improve something. There's lifehacking, biohacking, growth hacking, product hacking, and countless other examples of hackification.

- *Can a hack be successful at hacking? I think not. Can you hack a hack until he or she is no longer a hack? Please let me know if you've attempted hackhacking.*

B2B AND B2C

These are acronyms for the two major forms of advertising and marketing: Business-to-Business and Business-to-Consumer. Occasionally, you'll see some smartass write about how all of it should be "H2H" (Human-to-Human). I'm going to be that smartass right now. No matter what you're selling, or whom you're selling it to, resist the temptation to spew nonsense. Just try 2B yourself.

THOUGHT STARTERS

Most people can't think for themselves. Or that's what some advertising and marketing people believe about their co-workers. So sometimes, creative briefs and assignments come pre-loaded with "thought starters." The thought behind the inclusion of thought starters is that hopefully, the creative team will produce work based on the thought starters. That way, the person who first thought up the thought starters will start thinking he or she is actually creative.

- *Thought starters may be nice to have, but the advertising world needs more thought finishers. And thought doers. So help me, I think I've invented more crappy phrases just now.*

#BadCopywriterWisdom
Life is an email blast.
What's your subject line?

IDEATION

Some people are so busy generating ideas they don't have time to say, "idea generation." Or "idea creation." Or "idea bloviation." Whichever two words it's a mashup of, ideation is a word that's intended to sound more impressive than the act it describes. Not all the ideating results in great ideas, though. And be careful when someone says, "what we need is ideation curation." Hearing that kind of nonsense leads me to regurgitation.

- *To most creatives at ad agencies, ideating is also called "concepting." Be careful with the noun and verb usage, though. It's not called "conception." Save that for when the agency holiday party gets out of hand.*

EARNED MEDIA

Publicity.

MARKETING DEPARTMENT BABBLE

Of course, ad agencies aren't the only purveyors of new, improved, artisanally hand-crafted nonsense. The corporate world is rife with it. Clients — the marketers, the brands, the advertisers who embody Corporate America — are quite adept at dishing out nonsense in mass quantities. So here's a guide to help you keep up with the onslaught of verbal diarrhea.

PAIN POINT

As humans, we're all walking around in pain. We don't know it, though. Somehow, marketing managers have decided that all their customers, or prospects, are in pain. Lots of pain. So we all have "pain points." Aided by a marketing manager's bulleted list of "reasons to believe," their product or service is the balm that relieves the pain points. But, like scratching an itch that isn't there, it's a phantom pain. "Pain point" is a misleading phrase used to convince ourselves that the audience somehow quietly cries out for what we can sell them. My pain point is people who use marketing nonsense like "pain point."

THOUGHT LEADER

Back in high school, if you told people you were cool, you weren't. Same goes for calling yourself a "thought leader." If you have to go around telling people you are one, you aren't.

- *The same rule also applies to any self-professed "ninja," "guru," "evangelist," or "rock star."*

WHITE PAPER

Careful now. Show some respect. We're not talking about some ordinary report, a study, or an opinion. White papers are serious business. Unfortunately, many white papers aren't nearly as significant as they sound, and are full of jargon and subpar bloviation. Don't forget, paper towels and toilet tissue are nothing but perforated rolls of white papers, too. If you're asked to write a white paper, make sure it rises above the level of two-ply Quilted Northern.

#BadCopywriterWisdom
Life is a call to action.
So act now before this offer expires.

360-DEGREE MARKETING

Do you want to be surrounded by your deodorant? What if your supermarket just hovered around you all day? In a sense, that's what "360-degree" marketing means: Using all the media necessary to make sure that anywhere a consumer looks or goes, well, there's a brand. Yes, it's quite dizzying, this 360-degree array of media choices we have for clients to pick from. But don't forget, advertising is war, so assaulting people from all directions is expected these days. Frankly, I think the idea of "360-degree" marketing takes obnoxiousness to a new degree.

- *Other similar terms for using a variety of media in a marketing campaign include "integrated" and "holistic." If a client can't afford a 360-degree, holistic, integrated marketing campaign, the agency usually claims to believe in being "media-neutral." Which means "we don't quite know what the hell's gonna work, but whatever we can make money on, we'll try that."*

DECK

For a house, a deck is an add-on, but in advertising and marketing it's a must-have. Any presentation or concept needs a deck, which often gets created in PowerPoint or if you're fancier, InDesign. Like a deck of cards, marketing decks tend to be quite thick: I've even seen a 28-page deck used to present one email design to a client. So hours are spent writing and designing the deck. Then, because it's usually a rush job, someone needs to scrub the deck of errors. All this work often takes place at night or on weekends, when most non-advertising people are enjoying dinner and drinks with friends on their actual decks.

- *This is not to be confused with "all hands on deck," which means drop everything immediately for an all-employee emergency clusterfuck. And you definitely don't want "all hands on deck" on your deck. You'll be rewriting it for weeks.*

- *A deck isn't merely written, it's built. All those pie charts need craftsmanship!*

#BadCopywriterWisdom
**Life is a password.
Is yours unique?**

LEARNINGS

I had a high school history teacher who used to say, "You learn something new every day." I suppose if he was in advertising, he'd say, "Every day brings a new set of learnings." It's sort of a synonym of "lessons," but no one wants to be taught lessons on the job. So they learn stuff, or convince themselves they're teaching lessons for others to learn. When someone refers to "learnings," I learn how self-important they are.

- *How do you teach a group of people your learnings? It's simple: You schedule a download session. If someone misses the formal download session, you can impart your learnings offline. Where did people first learn to speak like this?*

SOLUTION

Sometimes, a product is just a product, a service is just a service, and a piece of software is just a piece of software. But that's not good enough for many marketers. Instead of being specific, they try to sell their product as a "solution" that will cure all. Don't fall for this. Insist on precise descriptions and promises. Customers will appreciate the candor because it's so rare. If you're determined to describe something as a "solution," odds are there's a big problem. And it's you.

DIRECT MAIL

This is a cute euphemism for "junk mail." Somehow it's more directly targeted to me because my name is on a list of double-jointed, martini-drinking cable TV subscribers. All the pieces of junk mail may have my name directly inserted to give them a sense of ersatz personalization, but they're mostly auto-generated, and I throw them directly into the trash. Why is it that a 4% response rate on a direct mail piece is considered terrific? Directly speaking, it's usually because the creative is crap.

MOVE THE NEEDLE

Obviously, advertising isn't much good if it doesn't have any effect. So any increase in sales, awareness, or prestige could be considered "moving the needle." You can't simply move the needle any which way. The needle must be moved in a positive, upward, or forward direction. So how do you move the needle if you have a difficult client who insists on hackneyed creative ideas, a limited budget, and a resistance to innovation? I don't know, but as the knitters might say, moving the needle under those circumstances is a tough needle to thread.

- *There's also "raise the bar," which refers to an improved level of thinking or creativity. But there's no direct correlation between creativity and sales. In other words, you can lower the bar and still move the needle. Many ad people have become quite rich with this contorted business model.*

CHANGE AGENT

Change doesn't need an agent. Or an advocate. Most people don't like change. But things just change, whether you like it or not. Go with it.

LOYALTY PROGRAM

Sorry, there's no such thing. I save 30 cents off a gallon of milk at Safeway because I have a plastic card on my keychain that says I'm a member of a "loyalty program." Nice discount, but it doesn't make me loyal. Any store that's cheaper, closer, or better will get my loyalty, at least temporarily. Think about it this way: You might believe your dog is loyal. But the day you stop feeding it and your neighbor starts is the day your canine loyalty program becomes a failure.

- *Is "rewards program" a better phrase? Possibly. At least it's more honest. People like rewards, discounts, and free stuff. You know, incentives. But please don't use the verb form, as in "we need to incent consumers to do something." Saying it that way that only incents me to hurl.*

#BadCopywriterWisdom
Life is a device.
What will you do with yours?

BEST-OF-BREED

I'm not sure where this phrase originated. Dog shows? Horse auctions? County fairs? However it started, Corporate America is now giving its products and services animal-like qualities. But beware of anyone who describes their company, product, service, or even worse, their employees as "best-of-breed." Even a "best-of-breed" Clydesdale is capable of taking a big dump in the barn.

- *You might think describing something as "best-in-class" is more appropriate. Trust me, It's not. If your product or service isn't universally known as the best, saying it's the best will fail to convince anyone. Go back to school and find some better descriptors.*

MONETIZE

Sometime during the dawn of our Information Age, we started coming up with business ideas or products that no customer would reasonably pay for. So we began to find ways to "monetize" these business models. In other words, make a profit. Which means either charging consumers for the product or service, or accepting advertising to subsidize it. Or both. You must prioritize the need to monetize. This especially applies to marketing-related ideas. Why? I have a simple rule: Someone has to pay for them. And someone has to profit from them. Otherwise, they're not gonna happen.

REAL-TIME MARKETING

Who knew that the Pillsbury Doughboy was capable of expressing thoughts on the Arab Spring? It's made possible by what's now called "real-time marketing." Any news item, special event, TV show, or unusual holiday such as "Talk Like an Australian Day" is now fodder for every brand to create a special ad to put on Facebook, Twitter, or Instagram. The trouble is, much of real-time marketing gets conceived and done in very little time, and forgotten in no time. Deep thinking and great ideas require, well, real time.

#BadCopywriterWisdom
**Life is a series of deliverables.
Are you adding value?**

ENGAGEMENT

Marketers are constantly harping about "engaging" consumers or producing "engaging content" with the goal of creating "engagement" with consumers. Which all sounds perfectly lovely until you consider that "engagement" is generally defined one of two ways: An agreement to get married, or a fight between armed forces. (OK, for some people they're the same thing.) Marketing isn't a marriage, and it's not a war. If someone keeps begging you to embrace engagement as if it's the only thing that matters (as opposed to, say, increasing sales), just break off the entire relationship.

- *If a customer decides they don't want to engage with a brand, or they decide to break off engagement, the marketer usually will do almost anything to get re-engaged. This involves countless emails, junk mail, texts, retargeted banner ads, and even phone calls. In other words, the marketer becomes a stalker. This is the mark of a dysfunctional relationship, or a brand that's just creepy.*

ACTIONABLE

Nowadays, it's not enough to change minds or attitudes. We need to provoke action. So we create ideas that are actionable. The problem is that, everything, technically, is an action. Ignoring something is an action. Telling someone to fuck off and leave them alone is an action. So be careful what you wish for, because your actionable idea may produce a bad reactionable. Reactionable isn't a word, by the way. Which shows you how stupid "actionable" is in the first place.

LOW-HANGING FRUIT

Let's face it, we're not monkeys or birds. We're first-world humans working in a white-collar industry where we sit around and make up stuff for a living. So naturally, we look upon the easiest, most obvious ideas as the most appealing ones. That's the "low-hanging fruit" in question. Sometimes they're perfectly ripe ideas, sometimes they're rotten. But for most lazy advertising people, it beats digging in the dirt to actually plant seeds of thoughts in the hopes of growing an original idea.

#BadCopywriterWisdom
Life is a push notification.
What message are you receiving?

ARTISANAL
HAND-CRAFTED

I include these not because they're commonly used to describe working in advertising or marketing, but they're overused in describing many products we see these days. Much like "shop" is used to describe an ad agency (as we discussed earlier), it's all too easy to present a product as being much more unique than it really is. To prove how excessively and mistakenly these phrases are used, McDonald's offered a Bacon Cheeseburger with an "artisan roll." Although to give them credit, at least they didn't describe the box the burger comes in as "hand-crafted" simply because someone closed the flap.

- *I'm sure by the time you read this there'll be another word that's in vogue. For example, a few marketers have co-opted "bespoke" from the fashion world. Don't speak about your marketing campaign using pretentious words like "bespoke."*

#BadCopywriterWisdom
Life is a SurveyMonkey.
On a scale of 1 to 10, how do you rank?

SILOS

I grew up nowhere near a farm but as I understand it, a silo is basically a big vertical storage facility for grain. Or soybeans. Or other stuff. The point being, you never put two different crops in the same silo. So when you hear an ad agency or marketer is "siloed," they basically have several departments that never mix. Which makes me wonder: On a real farm do they keep the chickenshit and bullshit in different silos? Because then you'd have a more realistic advertising analogy.

BEST PRACTICES

Another way of saying, "This is the recommended way of doing things." The problem is that it's never fully explained how anyone agreed to these best practices. No one says, "We tried some mediocre practices, and a few pretty good practices, but these are really the best ones." Advertising is a world full of superlatives and puffery, so best won't stay best for long. So in a few years I'm sure we'll be reading about "The World's Premier Practices" and "The Ultimate Practices." Please, I beg you, practice abstinence from using meaningless phrases like "best practices."

WHAT THE KIDS SAY THESE DAYS

Some phrases you hear around ad agencies aren't very specific to the advertising and marketing industries. But like black clothing and fauxhawks, ad folks have glommed onto many phrases that simply seem awfully silly upon close examination. And I must confess, I'm not feelin' some of the phrases people use these days, so I don't mind throwing some shade and dissing them. U feel me?

JUST SAYIN'

This is often used at the end of a statement when a person tries to say something smart or provocative but pretends it's an aside. They're not just sayin'. They're insistin'. Or they're just tryin' to rile you up. It's a CYA phrase for people who are full of crap and hope you don't notice it. And I'm not just sayin' that.

EPIC

Yes, every era has its way of expressing superlatives. From "23 skidoo" to "The bee's knees" to "cool" to "awesome" to "killer." Now, add "epic" to this list. Like all superlatives, nothing's as epic as it seems. If you don't believe me, consider this: Right now, someone's Instagramming their "epic" Arby's sandwich, which only seems tasty because they got epically stoned a couple of hours ago.

FOMO

Fear Of Missing Out. The ad industry was built on it. In the 1920's, Listerine coined the phrase "Often a bridesmaid, never a bride" to suggest that ladies with bad breath would turn into spinsters. They invented some dramatic FOMO with that campaign. And we're still doing it. We've convinced people that if they're not always consuming something, they're incomplete. Mostly, it's because we have Fear Of Missing Sales Targets. No mo' FOMO, please.

BLOWIN' UP

Here's another nonsensical war-like phrase. Essentially, destroying something now means creating something. And an increase in popularity is substituted for the destruction of population or property. But remember, just because you blow out an idea doesn't mean it'll blow up.

KILLIN' IT

Are you "killin' it" at your job? If so, is your office a blood-stained mess? Did you bury it after you killed it? Gonna hold a funeral for it? With some pallbearers, a eulogy, and an Irish wake? Oh, that's right — if you're killin' it, that's a good thing, no matter what "it" is. I suppose sometimes you have to go all the way. "I'm beatin' it," "I'm molestin' it," and "I'm wounding it but it'll probably make a recovery" won't suffice. Once again, we're equating murder to success, and that's a bit much for a white-collar job, I think. Let's kill this phrase dead, shall we?

- *Is it better to say, "I'm crushin' it?" That sounds a bit less murderous, although there's still an element of destruction-as-success here. As much as we love to pay homage to our hunter-gatherer ancestors, I still think it sounds silly when we use these phrases. Besides, often the most physical thing advertising and marketing people are capable of crushing are the Venti Starbucks cups they hold in their hands.*

NEW WORDS & PHRASES

Sometimes I find myself at a loss for words. (For a copywriter in advertising this is not a good career move, trust me.) Mostly, there are some ideas and phenomena in the business that deserve their own terminology. So I have a few I'd like to offer up. If they blow up and go viral, well, that'd be killer.

BRANDGASM

A term applied to any ad agency's proprietary, often trademarked process for doing research, strategy, and planning for their accounts. They're highly touted on agency websites and in new business credentials books but never really used in any practical matter. BrandGasms were invented to fool clients who don't want to know their million-dollar ad budget is riding on an idea that popped into someone's head while taking a shower. Any agency can have a BrandGasm, and some even have multiple BrandGasms. But all agencies are faking them.

AWARD LOSER

This applies to anyone who hasn't won many advertising creativity awards, yet likes or rejects concepts based on guessing what an award show judge would think of the idea. Award Losers are notorious for saying things like "That concept's not an award-winning ad." "What would show judges think of that?" "That's a bronze, but we really need a gold." Often times, Award Losers will pull a One Show book off the shelf or find a great TV spot on YouTube and say, "This is what we ought to do."

TAGLINE DEPENDENCY SYNDROME (TDS)

Describes any highly conceptual, often visually-oriented ad that doesn't make any sense whatsoever until you read or hear the brand's tagline. Symptoms of TDS include a justification of the idea such as, "Consumers often like to complete the circle themselves" or "It's better to keep them guessing until the payoff at the end of the ad." Books from ad school graduates are often infected with many cases of TDS. But just like cholesterol, TDS comes in both good and bad forms. Before you do any heavy concepting, ask your Creative Director if TDS is right for your work.

RETROACTIVE CREATIVE DIRECTOR (RCD)

Synonymous with the phrase "Monday Morning Quarterback," the RCD doesn't offer much feedback or creative direction on concepts — until they're produced and out the door. Then the RCD comes along a few months later to blame the underlings responsible for the concept by saying, "Oh, I didn't like that campaign you did," even though the RCD approved it.

CREATIVE DIAPER

This applies to any creative brief that has way too much shit in it. Like 7 or 8 primary objectives. Or a "single sentence" that feels like 3 sentences. Creative Diapers should be thrown away immediately in favor of a fresh, uncluttered one. But like all diapers, no one wants to touch it.

CONCEPTIWRAP

A quick summary of what just transpired in a writer/art director concepting session. Often used to validate a 3-hour pool playing session where a few notes got scribbled on a sketchpad. Example: "We got a good start. I think there are some good nuggets here."

MARKETING SUBHUMANAGER

A client, typically entry-level or mid-level, who possesses the authority to kill any work he/she doesn't like or "get," but lacks the authority to approve any work. Often they'll say, "I need to go present this to so-and-so," which means the concept won't be presented with any enthusiasm or skill at all and will die a horrible, premature death.

YESSHOPPING

When you have a great idea, or any idea, not everyone will like it. So there's a natural desire to shop it around until someone says, "Yes. Go do it!" As a copywriting teacher, I've seen students contort their faces in countless ways in the hopes I'll bless their not-so-great ad concept that they can put in their book. We all try to shop around (or hop around) for a "yes," whether it's from a Creative Director or the many layers of management in a corporate marketing department.

- *"Yesshopping" is often a means to keep raw ideas alive. Remember: Just like executions, your ideas may be randomly killed by people you've never met for reasons that don't make sense.*

PITY PATTER

The awkward small talk you have to make with the people in your office you don't know well — and don't really care about. Like the nerdy IT guy or the accounting person who sits at the other end of the hall. Pity Patter takes place largely in the office kitchen or during holiday parties. It tends to involve forced, inane discussions simply because awkward silences are even worse. Common Pity Patter topics include: Sick children; last night's game; how tired you are on Monday and how glad you'll be on Friday; and "What's that stench coming from the microwave?"

ABOUT THE AUTHOR

Once called "a philosopher king on all manners ad-related," Dan Goldgeier is currently a Seattle-based advertising copywriter with experience at small and large ad agencies throughout America.

A graduate of the University of Georgia and The Creative Circus, Dan is also an instructor at Seattle's School of Visual Concepts, a regular columnist on TalentZoo.com, and a contributing writer to AdPulp.com, one of the ad industry's most widely read blogs.

Follow him on Twitter at **@dangoldgeier**

Please send all feedback, comments, inquiries, and lucrative job offers to **dan@dangoldgeier.com**.

Made in the USA
San Bernardino, CA
15 September 2018